# JAKE AND THE SNAKE

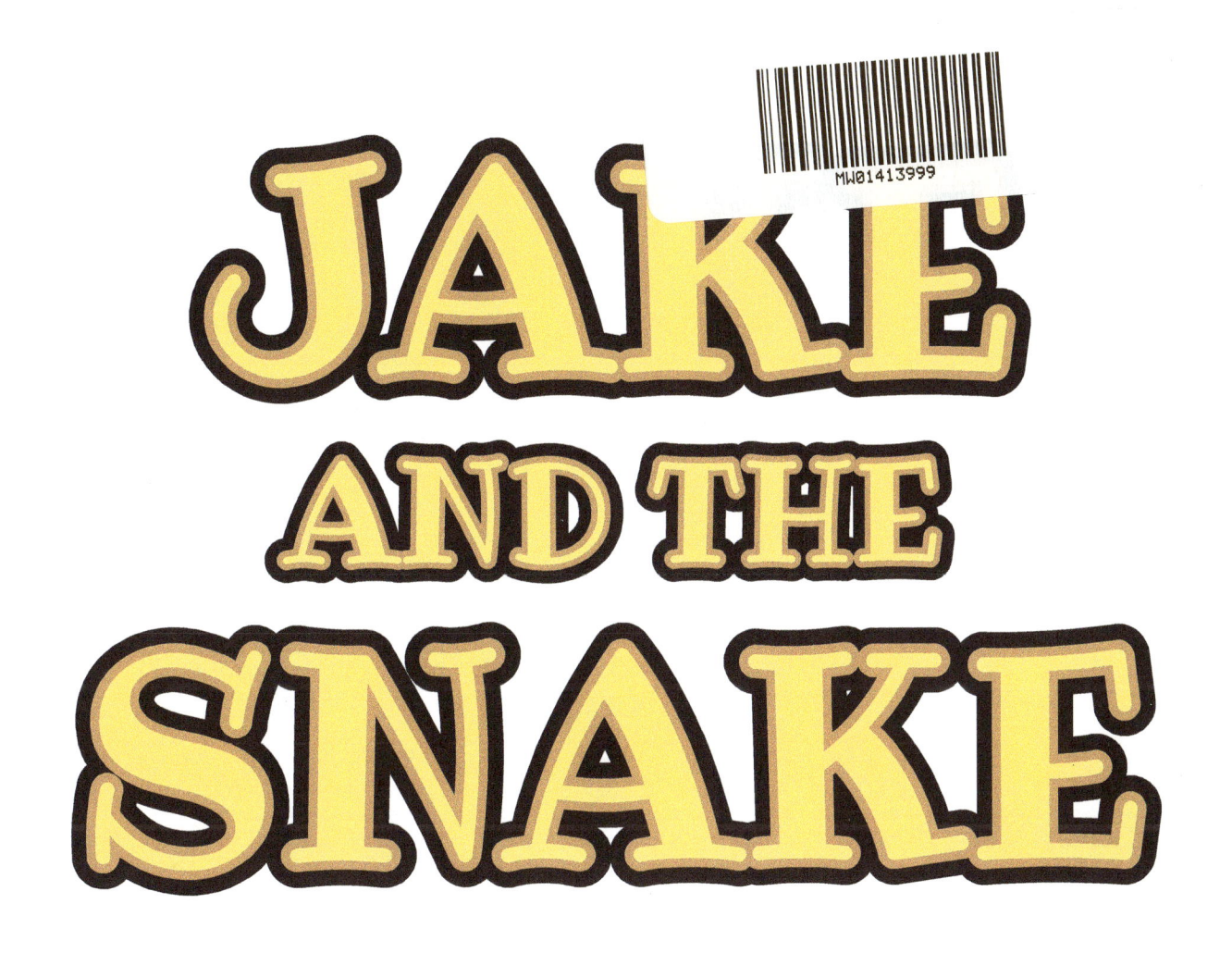

JIMMY BRIGHT

1

# JAKE AND THE SNAKE

This book is dedicated to the Creator God.

From Thinkbabynames.com:
Jake as a boy's name is pronounced *jayk*. It is of English origin. Short form of Jacob, well-used as an independent name.

Related forms via Jacob Iago, Iakob, Iakov, Jaap, Jack, Jackie, Jacko, Jackob, Jacky, Jaco, Jago, Jaime, Jakeb, Jakie, Jakob, Jakobe, Jakov, Jakub, James, Jamey, Jamie, Jamsey, Jay, Jayme, Jeb, Jim, Kapel, Yakov, Yakup.

ISBN 979-8-88540-186-9 (paperback)
ISBN 979-8-88751-389-8 (hardcover)
ISBN 979-8-88540-187-6 (digital)

Copyright © 2022 by Jimmy Bright

All rights reserved. No part of this publication may be reproduced, distributed, or transmitted in any form or by any means, including photocopying, recording, or other electronic or mechanical methods without the prior written permission of the publisher. For permission requests, solicit the publisher via the address below.

Christian Faith Publishing
832 Park Avenue
Meadville, PA 16335
www.christianfaithpublishing.com

Printed in the United States of America

My Father has a servant named Jake.
There was not anything that Jake could not make.

# SUF GANI YAH

Jake could really bake a cake.

5

Jake played hard and would sometimes take a break.

This story is about the servant Jake.

7

There was nothing about Jake that was fake.

From the time Jake would wake, he worked hard to make.

9

It was never thought by Jake to take or make anything fake.

Jake would never serve anything fake or take.

This is the story about the servant Jake.

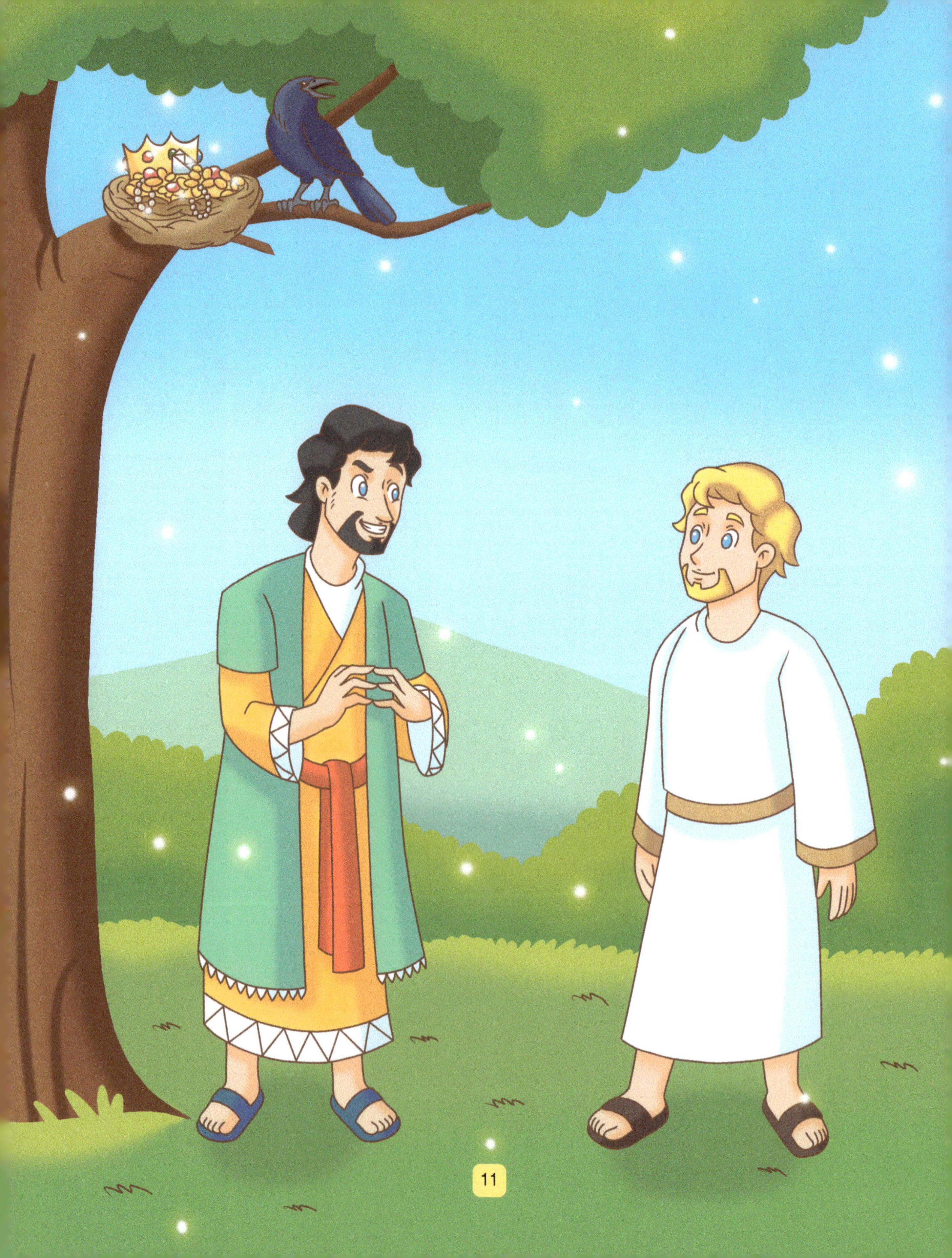

Now Jake knew a fellow named Zake.
Know that Zake served the fake.

13

Once Zake said to Jake, "You work hard and seldom take break.

15

If you serve the fake, you can always take break."
This is the story about the servant Jake.

17

One day Jake was working at the lake.
When the time came for Jake to take break, the man Zake appeared to Jake as a snake.
The snake told Jake that he should not work to make,
But that he should be a fake and take.

19

"But I love to serve the Maker and bake and rake," said Jake.

This is the story about the servant Jake.

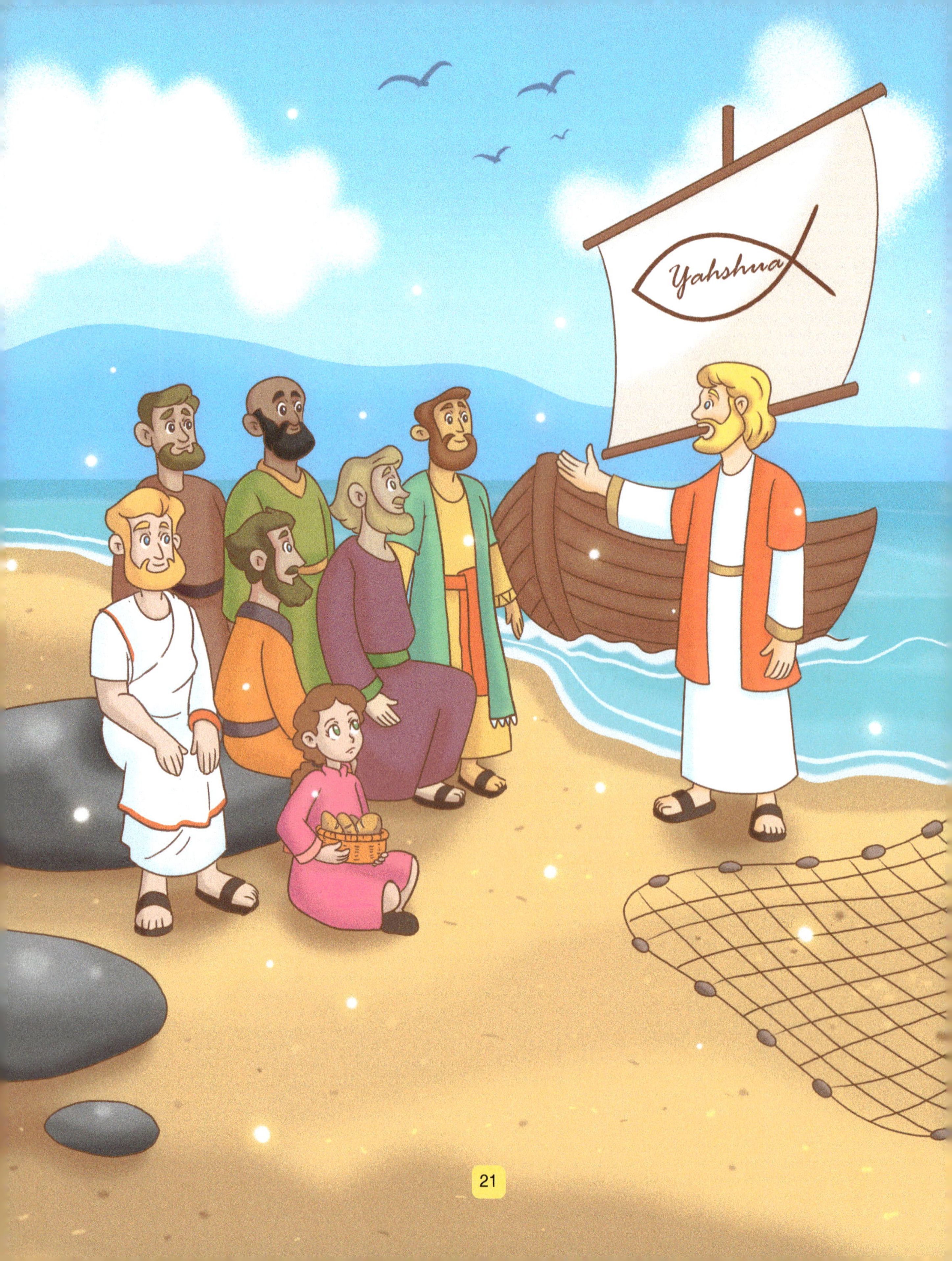
Yahshua

The servant Jake cried out, "I rebuke the snake for heaven's sake.

I shall not take or serve the fake like the snake."

So that day down by the lake,

Jake vowed to always make and to never serve the fake.

The LORD bless thee, and keep thee:
The LORD make his face shine upon thee,
and be gracious unto thee:
The LORD lift up his countenance upon thee,
and give thee peace.

My Father was very pleased with the servant Jake.

This is the story about the loyal servant Jake.

# About the Author

Mr. Bright is a graduate of Athens State University with BS degrees in accounting and computer science. Mr. Bright has worked as an engineer and observed many examples of successful processes and other processes which simply do not work. Usually the cause of unsuccessful processes is shortcuts and quick fixes that seem beneficial on the surface but will eventually result in failure or worse. He and his wife, Susan, live in Western Maryland, tending to the various animals on their farm and numerous cats. Working in the rural countryside offers the unique opportunity to observe animals and the sometimes identifiable human traits which they possess. The snake is persistent and patient. The snake is hypnotic, relentless in its pursuit of prey. The end result is the poor victim being unaware of the real danger until the last moment. Oftentimes this type of observation can be personified in animal characters, and this book attempts to teach a moral truth about the very real dangers one will face throughout this life and how best to overcome them.

CPSIA information can be obtained
at www.ICGtesting.com
Printed in the USA
JSHW062102171222
35001JS00004B/27